Haikus for Law Students

Jacob Erez

Haikus for Law Students
Copyright © 2017 by Jacob Erez

ISBN-13: 978-1541116009
ISBN-10: 1541116003

Interior Formatting by Streetlight Graphics

Disclaimer:
This book is written for your entertainment only. IT IS BY NO MEANS A LEGAL REFERENCE OR SOURCE. While I tried my very best to uphold the integrity of the haikus by researching any law they may refer to, by their very nature haikus are much too short to provide legal guidance of any kind or a comprehensive summary of any case, statute, code, or common law. Please don't cite the haikus on any legal brief, memo, or exam.

Introduction

HAIKUS. THEY CAN BE SO magical. To me, the beauty and power of a haiku is how it can portray an idea in a brief, but *captivating* way. When reading haikus, it's hard not to appreciate how much thought and emotion can be expressed in only seventeen syllables.

Haikus can be clever, witty, or serious. They can be funny or educational, or both. But whatever the tone, whatever the topic, they must conform to certain rules.

After two and half years in law school, I've come to value haikus even more. Why? Because an essential part of being a lawyer is learning how to communicate in a concise, clear, and unforgettable way. Your message must impress and convince the judge, jury, law clerk, media, client or Congress. And that's hard to do without *a modicum of wit and a poetic lens.*

In law, an attorney's brevity of language must convey a very complex idea, but also follow rules, just like a haiku. Looking at it this way, the work of an attorney is strikingly similar to a compelling haiku.

And while lawyers are less restricted by literary form and structure, there are many examples in law where pithy sentences can summarize and persuade at even the highest levels. Here are just two examples:

S.G. Tallentyre, in 1906, wrote this famous quote in The Friends of Voltaire:

> *"I wholly disapprove of what you say, but I will defend to the death your right to say it."*

In just nineteen words, the author sums up not just (part of) the First Amendment to the Constitution, but also perhaps, the *spirit* of American law.

Jonny Cochran, in 1995, poetically told the jury in the O.J. Simpson trial:

"If it doesn't fit, you must acquit."

And acquit the jury did.

That's the power of words used in a succinct, persuasive style; and that's what haikus are all about.

Perhaps then, law students and lawyers can practice and refine their craft by reading, writing, and loving haikus.

Jacob Erez
J.D. Candidate, 2017
San Francisco,
January 5, 2017

When an attorney
speaks with a poet's language
law becomes an art

Acknowledgments

I WOULD LIKE TO THANK MY law school, UC Hastings, for providing me with a terrific legal education. I have too many wonderful professors I could mention, so let me just acknowledge the fact that all of you teach with amazing passion, breath of knowledge and sincerity. Thank you. Thank you. Thank you.

I would like to thank Serena Aisenman and Sam Gutin for your help with the writing, editing and research necessary for the accuracy, clarity and humor of the haikus. You're both brilliant. Thank you to Donna Levin, Flutra Kasimi, and Nathan Suissa for help with the cover.

Big thank you to the folks at www. howmanysyllables.com, for obvious reasons!

Lastly, let me thank you, the reader, who

decided to attend law school despite the challenges; despite the rumors about the job market, despite the cost, despite the three years you need to devote to it, and despite the fact that there are those 50% of lawyers who give the other 50% a bad name (but I know *you'll* be in the right 50%).

Jacob

Haikus for Law Students

Jacob Erez

Orientation

look to your left, look to your

right – I'm on the aisle

First day of 1L

look to your left, right, and see

back of your peer's heads

First day of law school

What? Not what you expected?

There's no logic games

*F*irst day of law school

huge exam is coming up

bar prep begins now

Fast food negligence

the coffee was way too hot

you knew or should have

Wait don't eat that boy

it's not a necessity

Queen's gonna get you

Damn scale hit my head!

You were the proximate cause

now I missed my train

Rule 11(b)

file frivolous law suits get

motion for sanctions

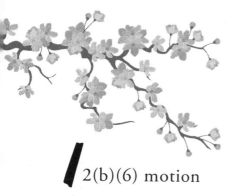

2(b)(6) motion

for failure to state a claim

your pleading is lame

I'm not listening!

don't turn your bank heist into

a conspiracy

Nephew please swear off

drinks smokes billiards cussing too

consideration

You breached your contract

make sure you remedy that

who needs hairy hands?

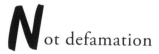ot defamation

when I said you're an asshole

I wasn't lying

First day Property

pursuit alone vests no rights

hey Post, that's my fox

Who the hell are you?

you have no right to pass here

got an easement sir?

Homicide degrees

Was it premeditated?

Or were you just mad?

*C*ausation can wait

you shot him now he's dying

a year and a day

*B*urglar or robber?

The difference between them

is like night and day

*C*riminal intent

general or specific?

Mugger's got no clue

Was on-call today

went much better than I'd hoped

professor was sick

Got called on today

just kept saying "it depends"

I think I nailed it

*S*tate the law, she says

but the law is in dispute

professor knew that

*S*ocratic Method

endless questions but never

definite answers

Rylands v. Fletcher

see to it that he's secure

that's a big lion

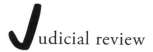
Judicial review

Madison v. Marbury

welcome Supreme Court

Who the hell shot me?

I can sue you both, you know

ask Summers or Tice

Damn car's wheels collapsed

what's privity, anyway?

hey Buick pay up

Hey! You sunk my barge

is PL larger than B?

Hand over that check

*C*at won't move his butt

off my casebook – damn! Case was

so interesting

Liability

as an accomplice is not

the name of the crime

Torts developed through

lots of cases about trains

what are those again?

41

*W*ho cares he's just five?

Had substantial certainty?

Wasn't *Grandma's* fault

What jurisdiction?

ain't my home state, read the case:

Home of the Whopper®

SCOTUS justices

I have to know all the names

sound smart at parties

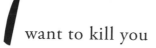 want to kill you

one Mississippi... BANG BANG!

premeditation

*C*rash injured your wife

now she can't cook your dinner

loss of consortium

Hey! Watch out up there!

Don't just throw your garbage down

got an eggshell skull

Law school progression

reasonable prudent man?

Now it's just person

Just a licensee?

No mutual benefit?

Please, enter my home!

*L*et's wrestle! Umph - ouch!

Man, I think you broke my arm

assumption of risk

Just a law student

you can't give legal advice!

Tell your mom and dad

*H*alf way through law school

on my way to a J.D.

does that make me J.?

Textbooks so heavy

this how Schwarzenegger trains?

I need a dolly

The Constitution

the debate is quite alive

and original

Used to be legal

not anymore but don't fear

no Ex Post Facto

*B*roke the law designed

to protect the guy you hurt

negligence per se!

You breached your duty

if I sue you will I win?

Try! But you're not hurt!

You breached your duty

who cares? No compensation

without causation

*C*onsideration?

No? But I relied on you

Feinberg help me out

Answering questions

when I haven't read a word

can I plead the fifth?

Art of networking

a LinkedIn® page early on

might find you a job

Going to law school

is like not having water

with your hair on fire

*F*uture goals are these:

graduate without any

alcohol problems

Dude you stole my car

you said it was a mistake?

Of fact or of law?

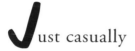Just casually

waiting for the bar exam

JK, freaking out

Protect your ego

please argue with someone else

we train for this stuff

Multiple choice test

much harder than just writing

"it depends" twelve times

I would consider

breaking my leg to get out

of taking the bar

*L*aw school all-nighters

have given me more respect

for coffee machines

*B*ought some study aids

but I've never read the case

that's on the exam

*T*wenty-four seven

study with all mind and heart

week before exam

3L finally

taking *only* twelve units

instead of thirteen

Now I find myself

using IRAC all the time

that's my conclusion

A hard tort hypo?

Easy solution, just sue

everyone you can

**N**egotiations

a subtle art form and skill

for getting your way

*S*upreme Court cases

essential for every class

dissents are so fun

*F*ound a summer job

what? They don't pay you at all?

No, it's Uncle Sam

Things law students love:

flawless notes, perfect outlines

it's the simple things

Top fifteen law school

graduated with good job

crippled with great debt

*W*inter break is here

time to catch up on some sleep

or binge watch Netflix®

Spring break reading list

no syllabus to follow

books I picked myself

While studying law

I've learned to appreciate

all brands of coffee

Writing legal briefs

should be in the Olympics

right after curling

*B*ring extra pencils

this law lecture is intense

might help to doodle

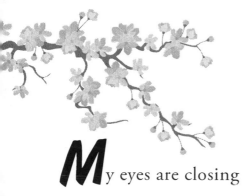

My eyes are closing

this law lecture is boring

catch up on some sleep

Possession is nine-

tenth of the law they taught us

that's enough for me

Blackacre is a

name of a fictitious land

where "A" lives for now

Myra Clark Gaines Case

would be as long as about

ten thousand haikus

You just shoplifted

sir are you under duress?

or are you just drunk?

*T*he law is largely

based on technicalities

that's my kind of right

Welcome to law school

ready to brief your cases?

Do it anyway

You can't take my land

sorry President Truman

Youngstown won that case

92

My dream was to be

Harper Lee's Atticus Finch

now it's Harper Lee

Wills and trusts are two

important documents when

you don't care; you're dead

*L*ady Duff-Gordon

a promise may be lacking

still got to pay Woods

*F*inished my first year

now I'm a "rising" 2L

where to I don't know

Law school is three years

insane amount of reading

lawyers read much more

Taking Evidence

makes them clear and convincing

my character flaws

Inchoate crimes are

not real crimes but somehow they

are still illegal

My agent screwed me

is Stambovsky current law?

who you gonna call?

I love learning law

expanding my intellect

and take-home exams

*D*on't need detriment

just a bargained for exchange

consider it done

Don't break confidence

represent client with zeal

do not get disbarred

No, you can't sue me

don't even try unless you

got some privity

*T*hree years of law school

can be trying – friendship is

key for survival

Mock deposition

eight hours of talking but no

coffee or pee breaks

*I*ncorporation

gives businesses personhood

a legal fiction

Minimum contacts

may subject a party to

the State their Shoe's in

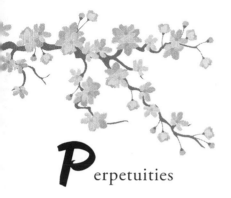

Perpetuities

we know there's a rule against

but that's all we know

A judge must apply

State laws in federal court

eerily enough

Barrel of flour

falls from the sky like manna

now *that's* res ipsa

Nervous in moot court

Your honor, may I begin?

Okay sure I'll wait

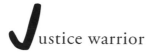ustice warrior

fighting for a righteous world

JK, studying

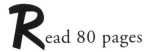Read 80 pages

highlight, brief, and memorize

then read 80 more

Law firm – summer school

schvitzing working studying

must be what hell's like

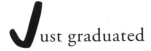ust graduated

time to pay my loans, but hey!

No more damn finals

Not Legally Blonde

better movie teaching law?

My Cousin Vinny!

Thank you for reading "Haikus for Law Students." It is my sincere hope that it was entertaining and educational, and that you found at least one haiku *so* fantastic that you'll quote it to your friends, family and professors.

If you'd like to contact me, please email me at Jacob.Erez.Author@gmail.com with any comments, questions, or feedback you may have – or just to say hello. I'd love to hear from you. Let me know what your favorite haiku was!

Jacob